Movie Stunt Worker

By William David Thomas

Reading Consultant: Susan Nations, M.Ed.,
Author/Literacy Coach/Consultant in Literacy Development

Marshall Cavendish
Benchmark

New York

Other Marshall Cavendish Offices:
Marshall Cavendish International (Asia) Private Limited, 1 New Industrial Road, Singapore 536196 • Marshall Cavendish International (Thailand) Co Ltd. 253 Asoke, 12th Flr, Sukhumvit 21 Road, Klongtoey Nua, Wattana, Bangkok 10110, Thailand • Marshall Cavendish (Malaysia) Sdn Bhd, Times Subang, Lot 46, Subang Hi-Tech Industrial Park, Batu Tiga, 40000 Shah Alam, Selangor Darul Ehsan, Malaysia

Marshall Cavendish is a trademark of Times Publishing Limited

All websites were available and accurate when this book was sent to press.

Library of Congress Cataloging-in-Publication Data
    Thomas, William, 1947-
        Movie stunt worker / by William David Thomas.
        p. cm. — (Dirty and dangerous jobs)
        Includes index.
        ISBN 978-1-60870-172-8
        1. Stunt performers—Juvenile literature. 2. Motion pictures—Vocational guidance—Juvenile literature. I. Title.
    PN1995.9.S7T46 2011
    791.4302'8—dc22
                                     2010000209

Developed for Marshall Cavendish Benchmark by RJF Publishing LLC (www.RJFpublishing.com)
Editor: Tea Benduhn
Design: Westgraphix LLC/Tammy West
Photo Research: Edward A. Thomas
Map Illustrator: Stefan Chabluk
Index: Nila Glikin

Cover: This stunt worker with clothing on fire was seen in the 1991 television show *Stuntmasters*.

The photographs in this book are used by permission and through the courtesy of: Cover: Everett Collection; 4: Warner Brothers/courtesy Everett Collection; 6: © Screen Gems/courtesy Everett Collection; 7: United Artists/Photofest; 9: MGM/Everett Collection; 10: © Mario Anzuoni/Reuters/Corbis; 12: © Warner Brothers/courtesy Everett Collection; 14: TM & Copyright © 20th Century Fox Film Corp. All rights reserved. Courtesy: Everett Collection; 15: Photofest/Paramount Pictures; 16: MGM/courtesy Everett Collection; 18: Paramount/courtesy Everett Collection; 20: © Buena Vista/courtesy Everett Collection; 21: © Walt Disney/courtesy Everett Collection; 22: Columbia Pictures/courtesy Everett Collection; 24: Hulton Archive/Getty Images; 26: AP Images; 28: James Fisher, TM and Copyright © 20th Century Fox Film Corp. All rights reserved. Courtesy: Everett Collection; 29: © United Artists/courtesy Everett Collection.

Printed in Malaysia (T).
135642

CONTENTS

b19367284

Words defined in the glossary are in **bold** type
the first time they appear in the text.

Fights, Falls, and Fires

The actors Christian Bale and Cillian Murphy pose during a fight that was mostly done by their stunt doubles in the 2005 movie *Batman Begins*.

A powerful kick knocks Batman to the floor. He is battling his former teacher, Ra's al Ghul, inside a subway car. Batman leaps up and throws a punch that slams al Ghul backward into a door.

Danger with Safety

That **scene** is from the 2005 film *Batman Begins*. Christian Bale played Batman. Liam Neeson played Ra's al Ghul. During parts of that fight, however, neither one of them was on the screen. Stunt workers, dressed as Batman and al Ghul, threw the punches and took the falls.

Bale and Neeson are famous, highly paid actors. If either one had been hurt, a lot of time and money would be lost. That is why stunt workers—sometimes called stunt doubles—perform much of the action in today's movies. They are the people who fall down stairs, crash cars, and get blown into the air by explosions. Their special skills and training prepare them to carry out these actions with less risk of getting hurt than an untrained actor.

Filmmakers want movies to be exciting and to look **realistic**. That means stunt workers must sometimes do things that are dangerous. Stunt workers do not take foolish chances, however. These men and women carefully plan everything they do. The stunts they perform most often in movies are fights, falls, and fires.

Taurus World Stunt Awards

Actors have the Academy Awards, often called the Oscars. Stunt workers have the Taurus World Stunt Awards. These are given out each year for the best stunt work. Awards are given for the best fight, best work with a vehicle, best fire, and more.

Samuel L. Jackson and Patrick Wilson stage a fight scene in the 2008 movie *Lakeview Terrace*.

Stitches and Broken Jaws

Movie fights look fast and **furious**. A fight that lasts just seconds on the screen, however, can take hours and hours of work. Every move is carefully planned. Each punch and kick is designed to miss—but only by an inch or so!

Actors and doubles rehearse, or practice, the fight in slow motion many times. The film **director** and **stunt coordinator** give them instructions as they practice. Many stunt coordinators used to be stunt workers themselves, so they know how stunts should be done. Every part of the

Stunt Worker Yakima Canutt

Eddie Canutt was known as "the man from Yakima" or Yakima Canutt. He came from Yakima, a city in the state of Washington. Canutt was a legend in Hollywood. In his most famous stunt, he was run over by a stagecoach and a team of horses without getting hurt. Canutt also invented many safety devices still used by stunt workers. He became a stunt coordinator after he could no longer take the physical wear and tear of stunt work. In 1967, he was given a special Academy Award for his work and for his inventions to make stunt work safer. (In general, there is no Academy Award for stunt workers.)

Yakima Canutt performs one of his famous stunts while doubling for the legendary actor John Wayne.

fight is performed before the action is filmed. But accidents still happen. Daniel Craig played James Bond in the 2008 movie *Quantum of Solace*. Craig did many of his own stunts. In one fight scene, he moved the wrong way and got kicked in the face. It took eight stitches to close the cut.

Even experienced stunt workers can forget their moves. John Foster has done hundreds of movie fights. He says, "The only time I got hurt . . . I leaned into a punch when I should have pulled back. I ended up with a broken jaw."

Baggies

In the first *Spider-Man* movie, Peter Parker, played by Tobey Maguire, is trying out his new "spidey powers." He tries to climb a brick wall in an alley, but he loses his grip and falls. Chris Daniels was Maguire's stunt double. On screen, it looked as though Daniels had fallen on the pavement. He really landed on a special airbag.

Today's stunt workers fall on a two-part airbag. One is inside the other. The first bag is soft. The stunt worker would bounce right off if it was hard! The soft, first airbag collapses, letting the stunt worker fall into a second, much firmer, airbag. That stops the fall safely. It sounds like fun, but it can be very risky.

Playing It Safe

Fortunately, most stunt workers finish a day's work without getting hurt. The work can be very dangerous. But because stunt workers are trained, know the risks, and use safety devices, most of the time they don't get hurt doing a stunt. In 2007, for example, fewer than 3 percent of stunt workers were injured on the job. (Overall, almost 4 percent of American workers are hurt on the job, not counting government workers such as police officers and firefighters.)

Paul Dallas had performed hundreds of falls. In 1996, he was filming a fall for a TV show. He had his own giant airbag set up, but something went wrong. Dallas missed

Burning Witches

In one scene in the classic movie *The Wizard of Oz*, which first hit the screen in 1939, the Wicked Witch disappears in a flash of smoke and flame. Margaret Hamilton played the witch. At the time, actors still did many of their own stunts, especially if the stunts weren't thought to be very risky. Hamilton was supposed to drop down through a trap door just as the flames began. The door didn't open, however, and Hamilton was badly burned.

Margaret Hamilton did her own stunts as the Wicked Witch of the West in the 1939 movie *The Wizard of Oz*.

A professional stunt worker shows what he can do at the 2007 Taurus World Stunt Awards in Los Angeles. Look closely at the protective gel on his skin.

the center of the airbag. He hit the edge, flew off the bag, and slammed into the ground. Paul Dallas died that day.

Burn

Stunts involving falls can be deadly. So can those using fire. In the 2005 movie *The Fantastic Four*, the character Johnny Storm turns himself into a **pillar** of flames. He is called "the human torch." Stunts where people catch fire are among the most risky.

For these stunts, a stunt worker wears a tight-fitting suit. It is made of fire-resistant material. The movie costume goes over the suit. A special protective gel is also used. It is smeared all over the stunt worker's hair, hands, face, neck, and other exposed skin. This stunt gel is made so it does not catch on fire, and it is very cold. The final step is to cover the costume with something that burns quickly and easily, like rubber cement. The director wants a lot of flames in a very short amount of time to avoid hurting the stunt worker.

When everyone is ready, the costume is set on fire. The stunt worker goes into action. People stand close by with fire extinguishers and blankets. Most stunt workers trust only other stunt workers with this job. A "burn" like this lasts only 15 seconds. When the scene is over, the flames are put out immediately.

Dangerous Magic

In movies, people fly, get punched, get hit by cars, catch fire, and fall down stairs. We know it isn't real. It's all part of the magic of movies. Stunt workers make a lot of that magic happen. For these people, however, the magic can be very dangerous.

11

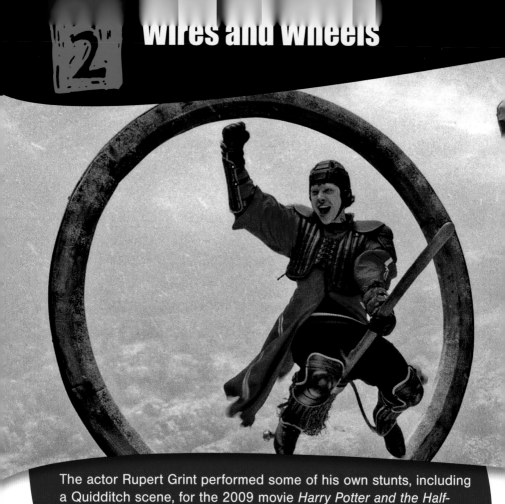

The actor Rupert Grint performed some of his own stunts, including a Quidditch scene, for the 2009 movie *Harry Potter and the Half-Blood Prince*.

"Not only are you in this **spandex** suit all the time, but you also have to wear this harness underneath the suit. So, I'm in that all day. Not only is that physically draining, but mentally draining," says stunt worker Chris Daniels.

Wires and Webs

Daniels was the stunt double for actor Tobey Maguire in all three *Spider-Man* movies. The spandex suit, of course, is the tight-fitting Spider-Man costume. The harness is what helps him swing through the air. The straps go around his legs, waist, and chest. Clips attach the harness to a wire, or **cable**. Daniels slides along the wire. He moves his arms and legs as if he were swinging from a spider web.

Daniels said his scariest moment as a stunt worker was in *Spider-Man 2*. "I jumped off a building about 200 feet [60 meters] on a wire. . . . That was the scariest, diving 200 feet and trusting that the rig was going to work." And it did.

Working on a wire is scary. It can be terribly risky, too. *Harry Potter and the Deathly Hallows* was filmed in March 2009. David Holmes was the stunt double for Daniel Radcliffe, the actor who plays Harry. Holmes was on a wire filming a flying scene. He fell to the floor and badly injured both legs. Another stunt worker had to perform the stunts for the rest of the movie.

Planning a Chase

Few things in modern movies are more exciting—or more hazardous—than car chases and crashes. To make them safer, cars are rebuilt. Steel "roll bars" are placed inside to keep the roof from caving in when the car turns over. Special tires, seat belts, and pads are installed.

Nearly all car stunts are done by specially trained drivers. Every step is carefully planned. For example, there

Stunt Worker Dar Robinson

Darren "Dar" Robinson was called "the world's most spectacular stuntman." He once drove a car over the edge of the Grand Canyon. As the car fell, Robinson jumped out and **parachuted** to the ground. He did movie stunts for 19 years and never broke a bone. In 1986, however, Robinson missed a turn while practicing a motorcycle stunt. He skidded over a cliff and fell to his death.

In real life, a car crash like this one could cause serious injuries. Stunt workers are trained to avoid getting injured in car crashes, such as this one from the 1971 movie *The French Connection*.

is a famous car chase in a police movie called *The French Connection*. It was filmed on the streets of New York City. The stunt drivers first practiced the route with toy cars on a large map. Then they drove the route slowly in real cars. Actual filming was done in short pieces and then put together. It took weeks to film the whole car chase. Stunt drivers are very careful people.

14

Car Cannons

In many chases, cars fly into the air and turn over. For some of these scenes, drivers use a "cannon ram." It was invented by stunt worker Hal Needham. The cannon is a metal tube placed under a car. Inside it is a thick pole and some **explosives**. When the driver presses a switch, the explosives fire. The pole slams into the ground. The force lifts the car and turns it over.

When Needham first tried his cannon, his car was blown 20 feet (6 meters) in the air. It hit the ground and

Stunt workers carefully plan the amount of explosives they will use to lift a car into the air and make it flip over. These cars were in the 2009 movie *Transformers 2*.

Stunt workers worked very carefully to make the car chase scene look dangerous in the 2008 movie *Quantum of Solace*.

Vampire Car Wreck

Actor Robert Pattinson did some of his own stunts for his role of Edward Cullen in the vampire movie *Twilight*. He said, "The scariest one was when I run, and I put my hand out to stop this car. . . . [T]he car went off its tracks." Pattinson was hit by the car, but not hard enough to be injured. And also not hard enough to be scared off. Pattinson again did some of his own stunts in the second *Twilight* movie, *New Moon*, which opened in November 2009.

rolled over eight times. Needham was badly injured, but he recovered well enough to use the cannon again. Next time, he used fewer explosives!

A Dangerous Business

Some of the best car stunts are in the James Bond movies. In the 2008 film *Quantum of Solace*, Bond's car was chased along twisting mountain roads. Six cars were destroyed filming the chase. One stunt driver was very badly injured in a crash, though the other people in the stunts were safe.

Car stunts are planned and practiced for safety. Even so, stunt driving is a dangerous business.

Candy

Lots of glass gets broken in movies. All of it is fake. Long ago, the fake glass used in movies was made from sugar and water. Actors called it "candy glass." The name is still used, even though today's movie glass is plastic. It shatters easily, without leaving sharp edges. Also, today's plastic movie glass won't melt under the hot lights used to film movies. Candy glass melts very quickly.

Actor Harrison Ford (left) wanted people to see the look on his face as he did his own stunts in the 2008 movie *Indiana Jones and the Kingdom of the Crystal Skull*. The other two actors in this scene are Shia LaBeouf (center) and Karen Allen (right).

If your mother saw you standing on the edge of a roof, what would she do? Tell you to come down? Cry? Call 911? Matt Epper's mother did none of those things. She yelled, "Just jump, Matt! Come on! . . . Just kick your legs out and fly!"

Ten-year-old Matt Epper flew. He sped toward the ground, landed on a giant airbag, and got up with a big smile on his face. His mother, Eurlyne Epper, smiled too. Matt was now part of a family of stunt workers.

Many Reasons

The Eppers have been doing stunts in movies for more than 80 years. Matt's great-grandfather did horse stunts in silent movies. His grandmother, Jeannie Epper, won awards for her movie stunts. His mother, Eurlyne, has done stunts in more than 40 movies. Matt's older sister and brother are already stunt workers. In one scene in the 2007 movie *Transformers*, a bus is ripped apart. Matt's uncle Richard was driving that bus.

People go into stunt work for many different reasons. For the Eppers, stunt work is a family tradition. Other people use special skills they have learned to get into the exciting business of making movies.

Cowboys, Athletes, and Soldiers

Some of the first stunt workers were cowboys and rodeo riders. Movie studios hired them to train and care for horses. Eventually, the cowboys started doing stunts. They

No Room for Fear

Stunt worker Hal Needham was once asked if he was afraid while doing stunts. "Is there fear? No, there isn't," he said. "Now, I've made mistakes. I've broken 56 bones in my body, and each one was a mistake. But when we do stunts, there's just no room for fear."

roped cattle, rode horses down cliffs, and jumped from one horse to another. It was a lot like their regular work.

Other people use their athletic skills to get a job in the movie business. Michele Waitman was a **gymnast** when she was in college. She says, "I got into stunts by **auditioning** for the Indiana Jones Stunt Show at Disney . . . Studios. I received incredible training there." Since then,

The actor Viggo Mortensen rode horses as a child. This helped him to do his own horse-riding stunts in the 2004 movie *Hidalgo*.

Waitman has done stunts for *Spider-Man 3* and the TV series *Buffy the Vampire Slayer*.

Jason Gray spent four years in the U.S Air Force. He was a **security** specialist, so he learned a lot about weapons. Since

Dangers of Piracy

Tony Angelotti was the stunt double for Johnny Depp in all three *Pirates of the Caribbean* movies. In the second film, *Dead Man's Chest*, he was badly injured doing a stunt fall. He nearly died. After three **surgeries**, Angelotti recovered. He came back to do stunts for the third movie.

Stunt worker Tony Angelotti did many of the stunts for Johnny Depp (right) in the 2006 movie *Pirates of the Caribbean: Dead Man's Chest*. The other actors in this scene are Jack Davenport (left) and Orlando Bloom (center).

Geena Davis does a split as she performs her own stunt catching a ball in the 1992 baseball movie *A League of Their Own*.

A League of Their Own

The movie *A League of Their Own* is about the women's professional baseball league that was formed in 1943. The league began play during World War II. At that time, many men, including professional baseball players, were in the armed forces. Some people then thought that women could not play high-quality baseball, but the players proved them wrong. The league was very popular with fans and continued for a number of years after World War II ended in 1945.

moving to Hollywood, he has done stunts in TV shows and movies including *The Mist* and *The Patriot*.

Stunt worker Debbie Evans turned childhood fun into a job. "I was a tomboy," she says, "the best at riding skateboards and bikes. Now I like riding motorcycles, riding them fast." Evans has done motorcycle stunts in more than 200 movies and TV shows. She has won four Taurus World Stunt Awards.

"Physical Acting"

Some actors want to do their own stunts. Geena Davis did her own sword fights and underwater work for the pirate movie *Cutthroat Island*. Davis also played all her own baseball scenes in *A League of Their Own*.

Harrison Ford was 65 years old when he starred in *Indiana Jones and the Kingdom of the Crystal Skull*. Ford did nearly all of his own stunts. He calls it "physical acting." Ford says, "I have picked up plenty of bumps, bruises, and cuts over the years." Why does he do it? "I think it's very important that the audience be able to see **expressions**," Ford says. They can't see an actor's face if he is using a stunt double.

23

4 Think About It Very Carefully

The actor and comedian Harold Lloyd performed his own stunts for the 1923 movie *Safey Last*. Here, he hangs from a clock.

Long ago, when the first movies were being made, actors did all of their own stunts. Buster Keaton, Harold Lloyd, and Charlie Chaplin were famous for their funny—but very athletic—stunts. They called these stunts "gags." That term is still used, though most stunts today are very serious. The people who do them have an exciting job, but they are very serious about their work, too.

Getting into the Business

How do people become stunt workers? Some of them want to be actors. They get into the movie business by doing stunts, and then they stay with stunt work. Sometimes they stay because they like it, and sometimes directors only want to hire them for stunt work.

Other stunt workers are like the early movie cowboys. They get into stunt work because they have learned specials skills outside the movie business.

Pilots are a good example of people with special skills. Lots of movies use pilots, especially helicopter pilots. Many pilots learn to fly in the military. Movie makers often need weapons experts, **scuba** divers, and parachutists. Those skills may be learned in the military, too.

Stunt Worker Jeannie Epper

Jeannie Epper's first movie stunt was riding a horse down a cliff. She was nine years old. Twenty years later, she was badly injured in a burning building stunt. "When I woke up in the hospital," she said, "all my hair was burned off." At the age of 66, she jumped through a plate glass window in a movie. Epper received a Lifetime Achievement Award at the 2007 Taurus World Stunt Awards.

At a stunt school in Seattle, Washington, the fire on a student's clothing is put out at the end of a practice stunt.

Even people with specific skills need to learn more, however. Today, there are a number of special schools that train stunt workers.

Not Your Average School

Imagine this. You walk into school in the morning. Your teacher says, "Listen up! This morning you are going to learn how to get hit by a car. This afternoon, you'll practice falling off a building."

26

It Doesn't Look Good

As a stunt worker, Glen Perkins plans fights carefully, so that no one really gets hit. Accidents do happen, however. Those scenes have to be done over. Perkins says, "For some strange reason, when you are actually hit, it doesn't look as good as when you're not."

At Kim Kahana's stunt school, in Florida, this really happens. Kahana's school is a special one for adults wanting to train as stunt workers. His students study car driving, falls, and more. They take classes in karate and boxing. Students learn to use firearms. They practice gymnastics, trampoline work, and climbing up walls using ropes.

Rick Seaman is a former stunt worker. He now runs a driving school in California. His students learn to do skids, roll-overs, and fancy turns. There are stunt driving schools in Florida and New York, as well.

Sooner or Later

All stunt workers must be athletes, and they need many different skills. Stunt worker Alison Reid gives this advice.

Watch the Action!

At Disney's Hollywood Studios (part of Walt Disney World) in Florida you can see stunt workers in action in the Indiana Jones Epic Stunt Spectacular. At Universal Studios in Florida and California, real stunt workers show how they do their stunts. You can even try some of the stunts yourself with help from trained professionals.

27

Hugh Jackman (left) and Taylor Kitsch did many of their own stunts in the 2009 movie *X-Men Origins: Wolverine*.

"Try to develop as many skills as you can—horseback riding, driving a motorcycle, climbing. . . ." Reid also says, "Think about it very carefully. Chances are, sooner or later, you're going to get hurt."

Today's stunt workers use careful planning, great training, and modern technology. Because they're well trained and so careful, most stunt workers have long and successful careers. Despite all the precautions, though, stunt work is still a very dangerous job.

So You Want to Be a Stunt Worker

Think about these things if you want to become a stunt worker:

- You need to be strong, flexible, and physically fit. Gymnastics, martial arts, and rock climbing are skills you may need. Horseback riding, **fencing**, sky diving, and scuba diving are important too.
- Some schools teach many kinds of stunt work. Other schools teach specialized skills such as race driving and working with explosives. Most of these are in California, near the movie studios. People must apply and pass tests to get into these schools.
- Stunt workers are always needed, though the number needed is small. When movies are being made, stunt workers may be hired on a daily basis or by the week. How much they are paid is often set by agreement between movie companies and **unions**. Most stunt workers belong to the Screen Actors Guild or another union.

Roger Moore played the role of James Bond in the 1981 movie *For Your Eyes Only*. A stunt worker did the real climbing up the side of a cliff.

GLOSSARY

auditioning: Performing to show your abilities when seeking a job such as actor or stunt worker.

cable: A kind of rope, often made of twisted metal.

director: The person who guides the making of a movie and gives instructions to the actors and other people working on the movie.

explosives: Materials, such as gunpowder, that will blow up.

expressions: The many different ways a person's face can look; expressions can show anger, fear, or happiness.

fencing: A sport in which people fight with swords.

furious: Very angry or violent.

gymnast: A person skilled in tumbling, jumping, swinging on bars, and other athletic events.

parachuted: Jumped out of an airplane wearing a parachute, an umbrella-shaped piece of cloth that lets someone come to earth slowly and safely.

pillar: A tall post or column, or something that looks like that.

realistic: Looking like something that happens or exists in real life.

scene: A short part of a movie or play.

scuba: Stands for **s**elf-**c**ontained **u**nderwater **b**reathing **a**pparatus; gear that divers use, including air tanks and tubes that let divers breathe underwater.

security: Protection from harm; safety.

spandex: A stretchy cloth often used to make uniforms and sports clothing.

stunt coordinator: In movies, the person who plans and directs stunts.

surgeries: Medical operations to fix or remove parts of the body.

unions: Organizations of people doing the same kind of work; unions try to get better pay and working conditions for their members.

BOOKS

Buckley, Annie. *Making Movies*. Mankato, MN: Child's World, 2006.

Hardwicke, Catherine. *Twilight: Director's Notebook: The Story of How We Made the Movie Based on the Novel by Stephenie Meyer*. New York: Little Brown Books for Young Readers, 2009.

Horn, Geoffrey M. *Movie Stunts and Special Effects*. Pleasantville, NY: Gareth Stevens, 2006.

Wolf, Steve. *The Secret Science Behind Movie Stunts and Special Effects*. New York: Skyhorse Publishing, 2007.

WEBSITES

http://debbieevans.com/videos.htm
Videos of stunt worker Debbie Evans in action on her motorcycle.

http://listverse.com/movies/top-10-memorable-movie-stunts
Video clips of some of the greatest movie stunts ever done.

http://omglists.blogfaction.com/article/105835/the-007-best-bond-movie-stunts
Video clips of stunts from the James Bond movies.

http://v10stunts.com/action_shots_8.htm
Photos and videos of women stunt workers in action.

About the Author William David Thomas has written books for children and young adults, software documentation, training programs, annual reports, a few poems, and lots of letters. He likes to go backpacking and canoeing, play his guitar, and watch baseball. He is the author of *Korean Americans* in Marshall Cavendish Benchmark's *New Americans* series, as well as several other books in the *Dirty and Dangerous Jobs* series. He lives in Rochester, New York.